Aberdeenshire Library and Information Service
www.aberdeenshire
Renewals Ho

KT-478-892

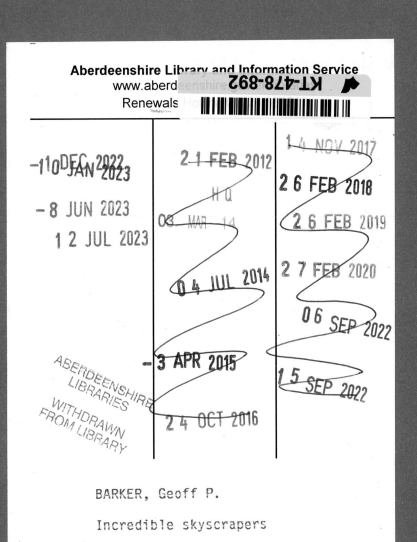

-110DEC 2022
JAN 2023

-8 JUN 2023

1 2 JUL 2023

2 1 FEB 2012

H Q

03. MAR 14

0 4 JUL 2014

1 4 NOV 2017

2 6 FEB 2018

2 6 FEB 2019

2 7 FEB 2020

0 6 SEP 2022

-3 APR 2015

1 5 SEP 2022

ABERDEENSHIRE
LIBRARIES
WITHDRAWN
FROM LIBRARY

2 4 OCT 2016

ABERDEENSHIRE
LIBRARIES
WITHDRAWN
FROM LIBRARY

BARKER, Geoff P.

Incredible skyscrapers

ALIS

2672007

INCREDIBLE
SKYSCRAPERS

Geoff Barker

W

FRANKLIN WATTS

LONDON•SYDNEY

First published in 2009 by Franklin Watts
338 Euston Road, London NW1 3BH

Franklin Watts Australia
Hachette Children's Books
Level 17/207 Kent Street, Sydney, NSW 2000

Copyright © Franklin Watts 2009

All rights reserved

A CIP catalogue record for this book
is available from the British Library

Dewey Classification: 720'.483

ISBN: 978 0 7496 8816 5

Printed in China

Franklin Watts is a division of Hachette Children's Books, an Hachette UK company.

www.hachette.co.uk

Editor: Michael Downey
Art Direction: Harleen Mehta (Q2AMedia)
Designer: Tarang Saggar (Q2AMedia)
Picture Researcher: Kamal Kumar (Q2AMedia)
Illustrators: Sibi ND and Danish Zaidi (Q2AMedia)

Picture credits:
t=top b=bottom c=centre l=left r=right

Cover: Jose Fuste Raga/ Age fotostock/ Photolibrary: Front, Ng Wei Keong/ Shutterstock: Back

Title Page: Lynn Watson/ Shutterstock

Underwood & Underwood/ Corbis: 4, Michael S. Yamashita/ Corbis: 5br, Kated/ Shutterstock: 6,
George Fischer/ CN Tower: 7b, Index Stock Imagery/ Photolibrary: 8, Lynn Watson/ Shutterstock: 10,
Jon Arnold/ Photolibrary: 12, Layne Kennedy/ Corbis: 13, Bartlomiej Magierowski/ 123rf: 14, Jose Fuste Raga/
Age fotostock/ Photolibrary: 15, Max Romeo/ Shutterstock: 16, Jose Fuste Raga/ Corbis: 17tl, Bill Croson: 18,
Jose Fuste Raga/ Corbis: 19, Mike Kemp/ Corbis: 20t, Fritz Hoffmann/ Corbis: 21, Sylvain Grandadam/ Age fotostock/
Photolibrary: 22, Superstock/ Photolibrary: 23tl, Michele Falzone/ Jon Arnold Travel/ Photolibrary: 24,
Louie Psihoyos/ Corbis: 25tr, Teo Huai Wei Edmund: 25b, Emaar Properties: 26,
Skidmore, Owings & Merrill LLP/ Renew NYC/ LMDC: 28, Madinat al-Hareer: 29.

Q2AMedia Art Bank: 5tl, 7tr, 9, 11, 17b, 20bl, 27t, 27b.

Every attempt has been made to clear copyright.
Should there be any inadvertent omission,
please apply to the publisher for rectification.

Note to parents and teachers:
Every effort has been made by the Publishers to ensure that the websites in this book are suitable for children,
that they are of the highest educational value, and that they contain no inappropriate or offensive material.
However, because of the nature of the Internet, it is impossible to guarantee that the contents of these sites will
not be altered. We strongly advise that Internet access is supervised by a responsible adult.

ABERDEENSHIRE LIBRARY AND
INFORMATION SERVICES

2672007	
HJ	2598258
J720.483	£12.99
JU	JNF

CONTENTS

EARLY SKYSCRAPERS

We think of skyscrapers as modern, tall buildings with lots of offices that house thousands of city workers. But many centuries ago, people also built tall, impressive buildings. Among these were massive stone churches with tall **spires** and **steeples** that stretched high into the sky. Today's skyscrapers rise ever higher, and some really do seem to touch the sky!

Steel revolution

The start of modern steelmaking in 1858 made the building of the first skyscrapers possible. During the 19th-century **Industrial Revolution**, huge quantities of **steel** were made. This light and very strong metal made a huge difference to the way large buildings were constructed.

First skyscraper

The Home Insurance Building in Chicago, USA, is often thought to be the world's first skyscraper. Built in 1885, this early giant was originally ten floors high. Two more floors were added in 1890. Sadly, it was demolished in 1931 to make way for another building.

*Built of **cast** and **wrought iron**, Chicago's Home Insurance Building also included steel in its frame structure. If it had been built of stone, it would have weighed three times more.*

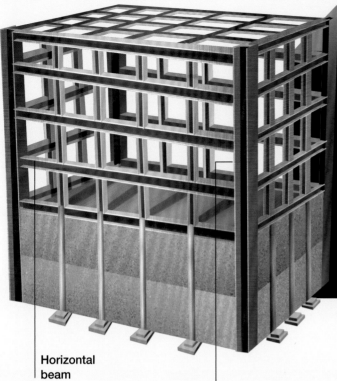

Horizontal beam

Vertical column

STEEL SKELETON

The science of skyscrapers is simple. Putting one floor on top of another is like stacking square wooden blocks on top of each other. The more blocks you add, the more wobbly the structure becomes. To stand up against strong winds, early skyscrapers used a strong steel skeleton of **vertical columns** and **horizontal beams** that were bolted together.

Wedge-shaped building

The distinctive 87-metre-high Fuller Building in New York City, USA, built between 1901 and 1903, is also an example of an early skyscraper. Although not tall in comparison with modern skyscrapers, it is still one of the most photographed landmarks in New York City. It is commonly known as the Flatiron Building as it fits snugly into a tight triangular space between two of Manhattan's main avenues.

New York City's Flatiron Building is wedged between Broadway and Fifth Avenue.

TOWER OR SKYSCRAPER?

A skyscraper is an extremely tall building. There are some towers, however, that are even taller than skyscrapers. What is the difference between a skyscraper and a tower? Skyscrapers are buildings where people either live or work, or both. Towers are not places for people to live or work in.

Eiffel Tower

One of the world's most well-known towers is France's famous Eiffel Tower (right). Designed by Gustave Eiffel, the tower was completed in 1889 in time for the World's Fair in Paris. It was made from wrought iron and reached a height of 300 metres. This made it the world's tallest structure at that time.

AMAZING FACTS

From 1889 to 1931, France's Eiffel Tower held the record as the world's tallest tower.

More than 200 million people have visited the Eiffel Tower since its **construction**.

In 1995, the American Society of **Civil Engineers** voted the CN Tower to be one of the seven modern wonders of the world.

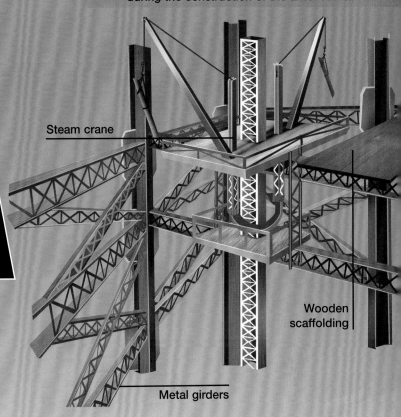

Small, steam-powered cranes were used during the construction of the Eiffel Tower.

Steam crane

Wooden scaffolding

Metal girders

Taller and taller

At 553 metres high, the CN Tower in Toronto, Canada, was for more than three decades the world's tallest tower. Its main pod contains a revolving restaurant and observation gallery, which visitors reach by high-speed lifts. But even this massive tower is now dwarfed by the 629-metre-high KVLY-TV mast near Fargo in North Dakota, USA. The immensely tall KVLY-TV **transmission antenna** has to be held in place by strong **guy lines** as it cannot support itself.

An elegant night-time lighting system was added to Canada's CN Tower.

EMPIRE STATE BUILDING

Number 350, Fifth Avenue, New York City, USA, is better known as the Empire State Building. This early skyscraper was built in 1931 and is world famous. In the film *King Kong*, the giant rampaging gorilla climbed the building, only to be shot at from an aeroplane and killed. The Empire State Building was the tallest building in the world for 41 years. In 1972, however, it was overtaken by New York's World Trade Center.

What's in a name?

The Empire State Building's name comes from a nickname for New York City. It used to be known as the 'Empire City', located in the so-called 'Empire State' of New York. Shortly after the Empire State Building was built, the USA suffered a severe **economic depression**. As there were very few new **tenants**, the building was called the 'Empty State Building' as a joke by New Yorkers.

- Height: 381 metres
- Where in the world: New York City, USA
- When built: 1931
- Designed by: Shreve, Lamb and Harmon Associates
- Materials used: Steel, limestone and granite

New York's Empire State Building contains about 10 million bricks.

Pavement attraction

Although 21,000 people work in the skyscraper, the Empire State Building is also a major tourist attraction. More than 120 million people have visited the viewing galleries on the 86th and 102nd floors. One of its greatest fans was French **architect** Le Corbusier. He said: 'I could lie on the pavement and look at it forever.'

Dominating the skyline

At a mammoth 381 metres, or 450 metres including its extended tower, the Empire State Building still looks remarkable today. It is currently the highest building in New York. Behind Chicago's Sears Tower, it is the second tallest skyscraper in the USA.

AMAZING FACTS

Construction work on the Empire State Building began in 1930, when 200 steel and **concrete piles**, or columns, were each driven 11 metres into the ground to sit on the **granite bedrock** below.

As many as 3,400 workers were sometimes on site at the same time during the building of the Empire State Building.

This early skyscraper was built ahead of schedule in a short amount of time. It took just one year and 45 days to complete.

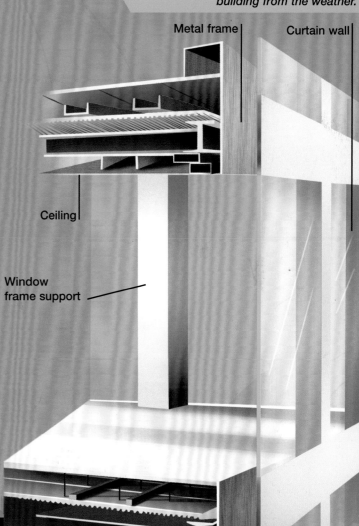

The curtain wall protects the building from the weather.

Metal frame | Curtain wall

Ceiling

Window frame support

CURTAIN WALL

A building's **curtain wall** does not support its weight in the same way that an outer brick wall supports the weight of a house. Instead, the skyscraper's outer wall covers the building's frame and protects people inside from the weather. The **Art Deco** exterior of the Empire State Building is made up of stylish **limestone** and granite panels. Like the curtain wall on many modern skyscrapers, this outer layer is also used for decoration. A number of modern skyscrapers have a curtain wall made of glass

SEARS TOWER

Chicago's Sears Tower became the world's highest building in 1974, and kept this record for nearly 25 years. In a city of high-rise structures, this gigantic skyscraper dominates the skyline. Sears Tower was designed by a talented team of architects and engineers from the city of Chicago itself. Skidmore, Owings and Merrill knew the problems of this famously 'Windy City', which has average wind speeds of 25 km/h.

Sears Tower's two huge antennae flash to warn passing low aircraft.

- Height: 442 metres
- Where in the world: Chicago, Illinois, USA
- When built: 1974
- Designed by: Skidmore, Owings and Merrill
- Materials used: Steel, with black aluminium exterior

Fierce winds

Sears Tower was designed to be 25 metres taller than New York City's World Trade Center's Tower 1, which at that time held the record as the world's tallest skyscraper. But its architects had to design a building that was not only very tall, but one that could also withstand Chicago's fiercest winds. Like the World Trade Center's famous 'Twin Towers', Sears Tower was to become a successful example of **tube building** design.

Four cross-sections of Sears Tower show the way floors are laid out at different levels of the Chicago skyscraper.

Floor 110

Floor 90

Floor 66

Floor 50

AMAZING FACTS

In 1999, famous French urban climber Alain 'Spiderman' Robert successfully climbed, without equipment, Sears Tower's glassy front.

From the Visitor Skydeck you can see Illinois and three other US states – Indiana, Michigan and Wisconsin.

Six machines are mounted on top of the Sears Tower roof to clean its 16,000 windows.

There is enough steel in the tower to build 50,000 cars.

'TUBE' BUILDINGS

The type of skyscraper known as a 'tube' building is built with huge columns and beams that are placed close together in the outer walls to form the frame of the building. The rigid outer walls make the entire building, in effect, a huge hollow tube. This has proved to be a very efficient design for a skyscraper. Sears Tower has a bundle of nine square steel tubes that form extremely rigid columns, with floors suspended inside the columns. The design narrows in steps as the building rises, and this helps to reduce the wind forces higher up the building.

Improving reception

In 1982, two television antennae were added to the roof of the Sears Tower. In 2000, one antenna was extended to 84 metres to improve local TV **reception**, giving Sears Tower a total height of 526 metres. Due to their height and position on the Chicago skyline, the television antennae are regularly hit by lightning.

Television antenna

Although the tallest television antenna on the Sears Tower stretches high above its roof, it is not included in the building's total height. Spires count towards the height of a skyscraper. Unfortunately for the Chicago landmark, radio and television antennae do not. Because of this, the Sears Tower is no longer the world's tallest skyscraper. However, it is still the tallest in the USA.

SOLID BEDROCK

The Sears Tower architects had more than strong wind forces to think about when they built the skyscraper. As the building weighs 200 million kilograms, it also needed extremely strong **foundations**. To get this strength, 114 piles, or steel and concrete columns, were sunk deep into the ground using powerful machines called **piledrivers**. The specially strengthened concrete columns had to stand firmly on the solid bedrock of the Earth to hold up the whole structure. Without these, the tall skyscraper would have started to sink into the ground under its own weight.

Light in comparison

The use of steel in the Sears Tower is very economical. Only 135 kilograms of steel per square metre were needed during its construction. In comparison, more traditional skyscrapers that have many supporting columns use over 200 kilograms of steel per square metre. In fact, Sears Tower compares very favourably with more modern structures. Less than 70 million kilograms of steel were used in its construction, and the building only weighs 200 million kilograms in total. This sounds a lot, but is less than one third of the total weight of Taipei 101 skyscraper in Taiwan (see pages 24-25).

Using sky lobbies

Up to 25,000 people travel up and down Sears Tower every working day. To cope with this huge amount of traffic, the company that designed the lift system for Sears Tower used areas known as **sky lobbies** to keep things flowing. Sky lobbies are special floors in which people can wait and change lifts. In Sears Tower they are found on floors 33/34 and 66/67. Here, people board and get off double-decker express lifts. From the sky lobbies, people can take any of the slower lifts serving individual floors to reach their final destination.

The Sears Tower's observation decks provide stunning views over Chicago's cityscape.

SHUN HING SQUARE

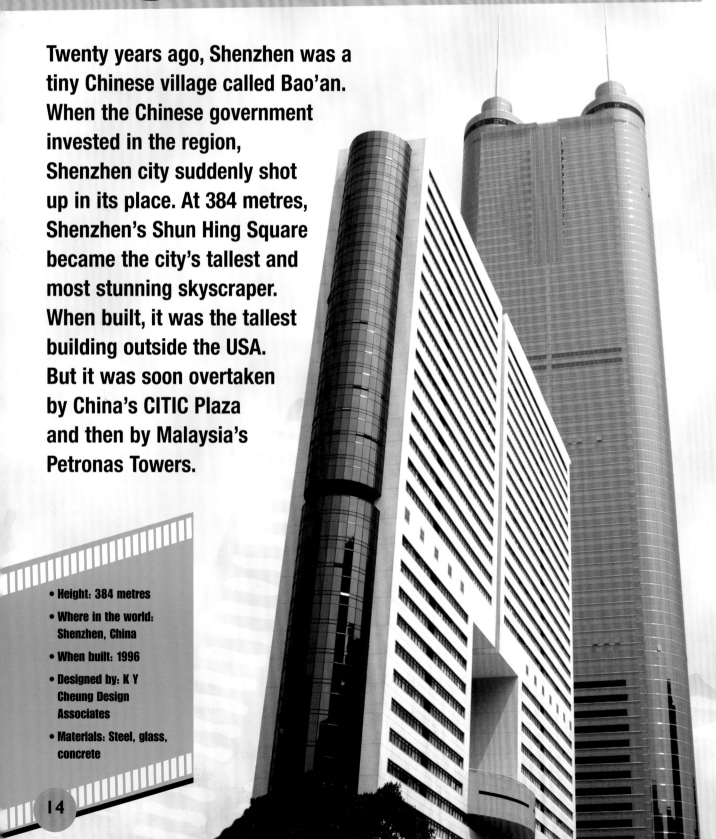

Twenty years ago, Shenzhen was a tiny Chinese village called Bao'an. When the Chinese government invested in the region, Shenzhen city suddenly shot up in its place. At 384 metres, Shenzhen's Shun Hing Square became the city's tallest and most stunning skyscraper. When built, it was the tallest building outside the USA. But it was soon overtaken by China's CITIC Plaza and then by Malaysia's Petronas Towers.

- Height: 384 metres
- Where in the world: Shenzhen, China
- When built: 1996
- Designed by: K Y Cheung Design Associates
- Materials: Steel, glass, concrete

Shun Hing Square towers above other buildings in China's Shenzhen City.

Skyscraper city

Shenzhen's skyline was recently voted as being the fifth best in the world. The city has over 20 buildings higher than 200 metres, and there are more going up every year. The Kingkey Finance Tower, which will be completed in 2010, will rise to 439 metres in height.

Distinctive spires

Shun Hing Square is a complex that serves different purposes. The main 69-floor office tower, with its two distinctive spires, has a public viewing gallery on its top floor. There is also a separate 35-floor building with offices, apartments and a five-**storey** shopping centre. Although Shun Hing Square is tall, without its spires it measures only 325 metres. Its highest occupied floor is 298 metres above the ground.

Typhoon-proof tower

The main office building of Shun Hing Square, known as Di Wang Tower, has a steel frame constructed of vertical columns and horizontal beams. It also has a **core** of **reinforced** concrete. In September 1999, **Typhoon** York swept across Hong Kong and Shenzhen. Although this typhoon had the highest warning level and lasted for 11 hours, Di Wang Tower's strong construction enabled it to survive the typhoon with ease.

AMAZING FACTS

The total floor area of Shun Hing Square is 273,349 square metres. That is equal to 27 hectares!

Shun Hing Square is the tallest steel-framed building in China.

During construction, four floors were built in just nine days.

15

PETRONAS TOWERS

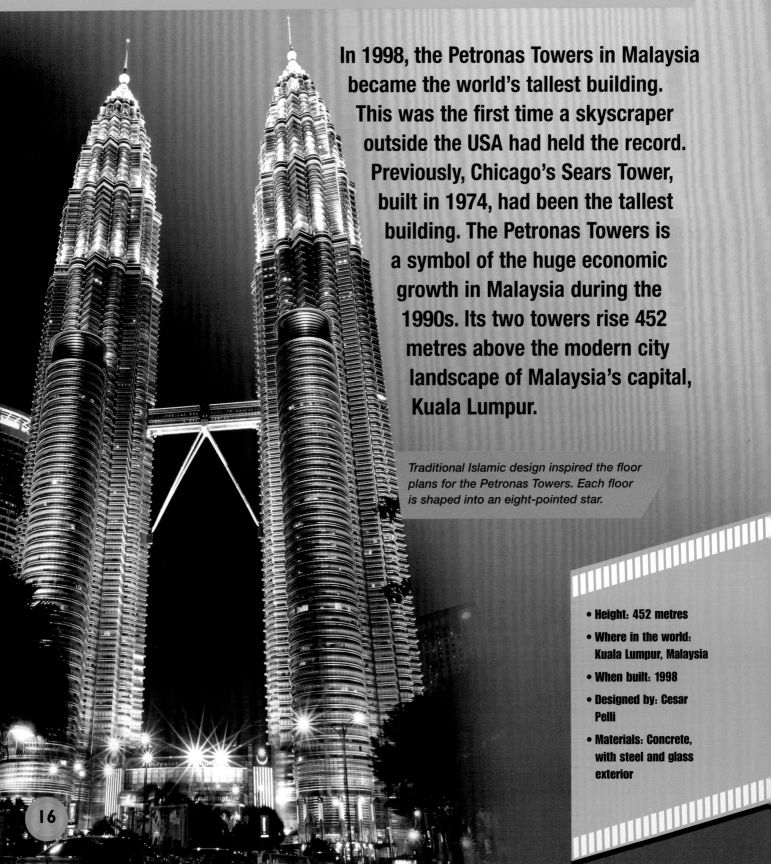

In 1998, the Petronas Towers in Malaysia became the world's tallest building. This was the first time a skyscraper outside the USA had held the record. Previously, Chicago's Sears Tower, built in 1974, had been the tallest building. The Petronas Towers is a symbol of the huge economic growth in Malaysia during the 1990s. Its two towers rise 452 metres above the modern city landscape of Malaysia's capital, Kuala Lumpur.

Traditional Islamic design inspired the floor plans for the Petronas Towers. Each floor is shaped into an eight-pointed star.

- Height: 452 metres
- Where in the world: Kuala Lumpur, Malaysia
- When built: 1998
- Designed by: Cesar Pelli
- Materials: Concrete, with steel and glass exterior

Bridge in the sky

The two Petronas Towers are connected by a **flexible** bridge at the 41st and 42nd floors. This sky bridge is 10 metres tall and 60 metres long. It was built in South Korea and put together on the ground at the construction site in Kuala Lumpur. The 650,000 kilogram bridge then had to be lifted halfway up the building to a height of 184 metres.

Leaning tower

One of the difficulties in building Petronas Towers was that two different construction companies were used to build each tower. A Japanese company, Hazama Corporation, worked on Tower 1, and South Korean builders worked on Tower 2. While Hazama had to spend valuable time in finding a solution to Tower 1 leaning 2.5 centimetres, the South Korean construction team raced ahead and completed Tower 2 successfully.

Petronas Towers' main lift systems are located in the centre of each tower.

Sky bridge

Structure 452 m

Foundation 120 m

Bedrock

Malaysia's twin towers were built on the world's deepest foundations to balance their great height.

AMAZING FACTS

If you don't stop on the way, it takes just 90 seconds to go up the Petronas Towers by lift from the basement to the top of either tower.

Malaysia's Petronas Towers featured in the 1999 film *Entrapment*, starring Catherine Zeta-Jones and Sean Connery.

There are about 16,000 windows in each tower. It takes a month to wash each tower, after which it is time to clean the windows all over again!

JIN MAO BUILDING

Jin Mao Building, which means 'Golden Prosperity Building', rises high above Shanghai's city skyline. Based on the style of Chinese **pagodas**, the building's **tiers** gradually taper inwards and floors become smaller towards the top. This building is important as it is one of the first of China's really huge towers.

- **Height: 421 metres**
- **Where in the world: Shanghai, China**
- **When built: 1999**
- **Designed by: Adrian Smith; Skidmore, Owings and Merrill**
- **Materials: Steel and concrete**

The structure of Jin Mao Building becomes more complex as it rises.

World's highest hotel

Like many skyscrapers, Jin Mao Building has several uses. There are shops and restaurants, while floors three to 50 are given over to office space. Jin Mao Building is also the world's tallest building containing a hotel. The five-star Grand Hyatt Hotel, which occupies the top 38 floors, has the highest hotel rooms in the world!

Need a lift?

It is not practical for a high-rise building to be serviced solely by stairs. People need lifts to get up and down a tall building. In skyscrapers, lifts are usually situated in the central part of the building. Jin Mao Building's lifts and staircases are found in the eight-sided inner vertical passage that rises from the ground to floor 53. The upper floors occupied by the Grand Hyatt Hotel's 555 rooms are serviced by further lifts that glide up and down the outside of the **structural** inner core.

Jin Mao Building (centre) is a key feature of Shanghai's dramatic skyline.

LUCKY NUMBER EIGHT

In China, the number eight is considered to be very lucky. This number crops up everywhere in the construction and design of the Jin Mao Building, which has 88 floors! The building's inner core of eight enormous columns acts like a spine for a skeleton. The concrete columns are themselves surrounded by eight columns of steel that help the skyscraper withstand powerful typhoons and earthquakes.

The massive *atrium* in the Jin Mao Building rises from the 56th floor to the 87th floor. It is lined with spiralling corridors and staircases.

Spiralling corridors

Structural inner core

Lifts

How does a damper work?

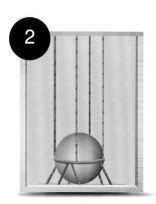

1

Damper sways left, counteracting a building's movement to the right

2

Damper is at the mid-point of its swaying motion

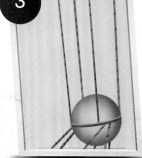

3

Damper sways right, counteracting a building's movement to the left

Counteracting sway

Jin Mao Building was designed to survive extreme weather conditions without suffering damage. The tower can withstand typhoon winds and powerful earthquakes. The Grand Hyatt Hotel's swimming pool on the 57th floor serves a vital function. Apart from providing entertainment for the hotel guests, the pool also acts as a **damper** to help reduce wind movement. A damper is a heavy weight that works to **counteract** the swaying of a building. With Jin Mao Building, as the tower starts to **sway** one way, the weight of the swimming pool means that the building moves more slowly. In effect, it pulls the tower back toward the centre. This limits the movement of the whole of the building.

High-rise tragedy

A huge skyscraper presents one of the biggest challenges to extreme sports enthusiasts. Famous urban climber Alain 'Spiderman' Robert successfully scaled Jin Mao Building in 2007. Tragically, BASE jumper Roland 'Slim' Simpson from Australia died following a jump from the top of the building in 2003. BASE is short for Buildings, Antennae, Spans (bridges) and Earth (cliffs) – jumpers launch themselves from these when they make a jump. They use a parachute or a 'wing suit' and a parachute. In the jump from Jin Mao Building, Simpson's parachute did not open properly.

Construction workers on Jin Mao Building needed a head for heights and steady feet.

AMAZING FACTS

Jin Mao Building has the world's longest **laundry chute**. It runs from the top of the tower to the basement. There are buffers along its length to slow down the speed of falling dirty washing.

In 2001, 31-year-old shoe salesman Han Qizhi was the first person to scale Jin Mao Building.

2IFC, HONG KONG

Architect Cesar Pelli won an international competition to design Tower 2 of the International Finance Centre, or 2IFC for short, in the heart of the city of Hong Kong. Strong and elegant at 415 metres tall, 2IFC dwarfed nearby 1IFC, which is 210 metres tall. With its 88 floors, 2IFC is currently Hong Kong's tallest building.

- Height: 415 metres
- Where in the world: Hong Kong, China
- When built: 2003
- Designed by: Cesar Pelli
- Materials: Steel and glass

Square central core

Builders erected 2IFC in record time. Its 88 floors were built at a rate of one every three days. The building's structure is straightforward, which helped to speed up construction. 2IFC has a huge, square central core made from reinforced concrete. This supports the whole structure like a strong backbone. To strengthen the core, there are eight steel and concrete super-columns and eight smaller steel columns. Seen from above, these supporting columns are arranged in a cross-like formation. The curtain wall is lightweight, and provides minimal support for the building. 2IFC was completed and opened in 2003.

Moving people

Double-decker lifts, in which one lift car is attached to the top of another, are an important design feature in many recent skyscrapers. These double lifts enable passengers on two different floors to move up or down at the same time, increasing the efficiency of the lift shaft. Double deckers work well in buildings where a busy single lift would otherwise be stopping at every floor. For a skyscraper such as 2IFC, double-decker lifts also use less inner core space than normal lifts for the same amount of traffic. This frees up more space on each floor for offices.

2IFC has 42 high-speed passenger lifts that operate in seven different zones.

AMAZING FACTS

2IFC featured in the films *Tomb Raider II: The Cradle of Life* and the Batman film *Dark Knight*. In these two films, the characters Batman, Lara Croft and Terry Sheridan jump off the building.

An advertisement was put up on the front of 21FC in 2003. It was 230 metres long and covered 50 floors!

TAIPEI 101

Opened on 31 December 2004, Taiwan's Taipei 101 was a fitting place to start the New Year celebrations. At 57 metres taller than Petronas Towers in Kuala Lumpur, Malaysia, Taipei 101 became the world's tallest building when completed.

- Height: 509 metres
- Where in the world: Taipei, Taiwan
- When built: 2004
- Designed by: C Y Lee
- Materials: Steel

Stick of bamboo

Taipei 101, which some people think resembles a giant Chinese pagoda, is a stunning high-rise that dwarfs surrounding buildings. The skyscraper's owners, Taipei Financial Centre Corporation, compare Taipei 101 to a stick of bamboo. That explains the rugged, tiered effect of the eight wider sections as the building rises. The Chinese consider bamboo to be very strong and flexible.

AMAZING FACTS

Why the number 101? The building is situated in Taipei's 101 district. It also has 101 floors!

Taipei 101 was the world's first building to break the half-kilometre mark in height. That is, more than 500 metres.

Taipei 101 contains the world's fastest **ascending** lift. It can reach the 89th floor in just 37 seconds, with a top speed of more than 60 km/h.

When the wind blows

An enormous yellow metal ball, weighing 660 tonnes, hangs in the middle of the skyscraper's 88th floor. This is a damper (see p. 20) designed to absorb wind forces and reduce swaying movements during extreme weather conditions. This is just as well, because Taipei 101 is situated in one of the worst earthquake zones in the world. There were also weather problems as the building went up. Five people were killed in 2002 when a construction crane fell during an earthquake. Now that Taipei 101 is complete, the damper should help the building withstand the very worst **tremors**, as well as typhoons.

Standing firm

A tall skyscraper has to be supported by firm foundations. During the construction of Taipei 101, up to 400 concrete piles, or huge round columns, were sunk into the ground to a depth of 80 metres. This was done so that the piles stand firmly on solid bedrock and will not sink.

The half-kilometre high Taipei 101 has the fastest lift in the world.

The massive yellow damper hangs down to the middle of the skyscraper's 88th floor.

Strong cable

BURJ DUBAI

In July 2007, Burj Dubai, or Dubai Tower, surpassed Taipei 101 and became the tallest building on Earth. Located in Dubai in the United Arab Emirates, this enormous new mega-high-rise has broken all the records. In April 2008, Burj Dubai overtook the USA's KVLY-TV mast to become the tallest artificial structure in the world. Burj Dubai is 818 metres high, over twice the height of New York's Empire State Building.

Living in the sky

Burj Dubai has 160 floors suitable for occupation. This includes offices and luxury residences, four swimming pools, restaurants, a fitness suite, an observation deck and a viewing gallery.

Y-shaped structure

Burj Dubai has a curtain wall made of glass and metal. The glass covers an area of 83,600 square metres, out of a total curtain wall area of 111,500 square metres. This massive total area is equivalent to 17 football pitches. The Y-shaped structure of the tower in cross-section makes the most of window area and natural light.

- Height: 818 metres
- Where in the world: Dubai, UAE
- When built: 2003-2009
- Designed by: Adrian Smith; Skidmore, Owings and Merrill
- Materials: Reinforced concrete, glass and steel exterior

The tip of the tower's spire is visible up to 95 kilometres away.

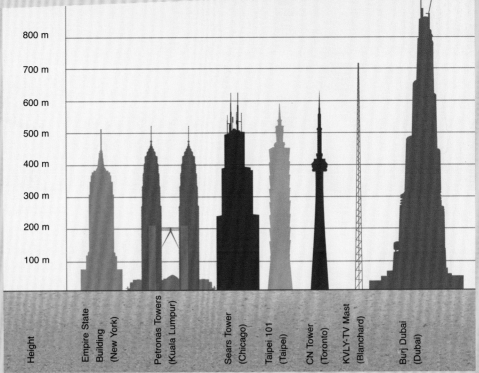

Height	Empire State Building (New York)	Petronas Towers (Kuala Lumpur)	Sears Tower (Chicago)	Taipei 101 (Taipei)	CN Tower (Toronto)	KVLY-TV Mast (Blanchard)	Burj Dubai (Dubai)

At more than 800 metres in height, Burj Dubai dwarfs other skyscrapers.

Tonnes of rebar

In its structure, Burj Dubai uses a lot of **rebar**, which is short for 'reinforcing bar'. Made of steel, rebar is usually formed from a cage or grid of beams, which is then **embedded** inside concrete. This makes reinforced concrete, which is much stronger than ordinary concrete. The tower, platform and office annex use 31,400 tonnes of rebar. Laid end to end, the steel rebar would stretch over one-quarter of the way around the world!

ADRIAN SMITH

Burj Dubai's architect, Adrian Smith, has worked for the famous Chicago-based company Skidmore, Owings and Merrill. This top architect has already designed Jin Mao Building. His inspiration for the spectacular design of Burj Dubai came from a flower called hymenocallis, as well as from traditional patterns in Islamic architecture.

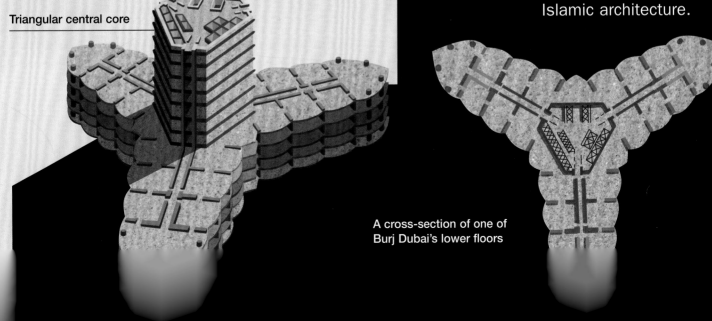

Triangular central core

A cross-section of one of Burj Dubai's lower floors

SKYSCRAPERS IN THE FUTURE

Burj Dubai is a landmark in the history of high-rise buildings. But there are many further skyscrapers being planned, some of which are already underway. Many countries are in friendly competition to build the world's tallest building.

Freedom Tower

New York City is recovering from the destruction in 2001 of the World Trade Center's famous 'Twin Towers'. Work on the foundations of the Freedom Tower, part of the new World Trade Center, began in 2006. Although the new tower will not be the tallest in the world, it will still be a huge 541 metres high. That is 100 metres taller than the USA's current tallest building. The new tower is due to be completed in 2012.

This computer graphic shows how Freedom Tower will look.

Sky's the limit

In 2008, Kuwait's government approved plans for a huge development called Madinat al-Hareer, meaning 'City of Silk'. The centrepiece of the new city is to be the Burj Mubarak al-Kabir, a skyscraper reaching a massive 1,001 metres in height. The futuristic city may take 25 years to build, but the huge tower is set to be completed as early as 2012.

Competing for the crown

Further proposed mega skyscrapers are the Mile-High Tower in Saudi Arabia and the Murjan Tower in Bahrain. Dubai, however, looks reluctant to give up its recent crown of having the tallest building on Earth. Plans are already underway to build Al Burj on a site within 25 kilometres of Burj Dubai. If built, the new skyscraper could be as tall as 1,400 metres.

AMAZING FACTS

New York City's Freedom Tower will be 1,776 feet (541 metres) tall. This figure reflects the importance of the year 1776 when the American Declaration of Independence was signed.

The Mile-High Tower planned for Jeddah, Saudi Arabia, may not be quite so tall after all. Although it was planned to be one mile, or about 1,600 metres tall, the massive skyscraper is more likely to be about 1,100 metres tall.

Burj Mubarak al-Kabir Tower will dominate the Kuwait skyline.

GLOSSARY

architect
someone qualified to design buildings and to oversee their construction

Art Deco
distinctive style of decorative art from the 1920s and 1930s

ascending
to be going up

atrium
open hall area inside a building, which may rise up several storeys

bedrock
solid layer of rock situated beneath the soil

cast iron
a hard, brittle form of the metal iron

civil engineer
someone qualified to design and construct public works, such as buildings and bridges

concrete
strong building material made using cement, water and sand or gravel

construction
building or putting up a structure

core
area in the centre of a building; strong column surrounding lifts and stairways and which supports a skyscraper

counteract
to act against

curtain wall
an outside wall that is not used for support

damper
heavy weight that helps reduce movement of a tall building during strong winds

economic depression
period when business activity and employment decline severely

embed
fix something firmly into something else

flexible
able to be bent easily without breaking

foundations
strong base on which a building stands

granite
hard rock sometimes used by builders

guy lines
ropes or cables used to steady a structure

horizontal beams
strong lengths of metal positioned across a structure for support

Industrial Revolution
transformation of Britain and other countries into industrial nations

laundry chute
shaft used to send clothes or linen down to a lower level

limestone
rock often used for building; also used to make cement

pagoda
tower temple with many tiers or storeys

pile
long column hammered vertically into soil to form part of a building's foundation

piledriver
powerful machine used to hammer piles, or strong columns, deep into the ground

rebar
short for 'reinforcing bar', a cage or grid of steel beams; this is then used to make reinforced concrete

reception
in TV or radio, the sound and/or picture quality of a broadcast received

reinforced
specially strengthened

sky lobby
special public area where people can wait and change from one set of lifts to another

spire
tall, pointed roof at the top of a tower

steel
strong metal used in building construction

steeple
tall structure at the top of a church or public building, ending with a spire

storey
floor or level of a building

structural
to do with the structure, or the way a building has been constructed

sway
movement to and fro, or swinging

tenants
people who pay money to live or work in a building

tier
layer or level

transmission antenna
aerial used for sending radio or TV signals

tremor
minor earthquake

tube building
skyscraper using a system of huge columns to create a hollow tube for support

typhoon
violent tropical storm or cyclone

vertical columns
upright pillars that help support a building

wrought iron
an easily forged and welded form of iron

INDEX

WEBLINKS

http://skyscraperpage.com/diagrams/
View a comprehensive collection of skyscraper diagrams, including ongoing and proposed constructions.

www.emporis.com/en/bu/sk/st/tp/wo/
Find out more about the world's tallest high-rise buildings.

www.motioneering.ca/Public/Taipei101Animation.aspx
See how the tuned mass damper works at Taipei 101.

www.pbs.org/wgbh/buildingbig/lab/forces.html
Watch animations of how different forces can affect a skyscraper.

www.pbs.org/wgbh/buildingbig/skyscraper/basics.html
This excellent website will give you all the important basics about skyscrapers.